GOD'S MEDICINE BOTTLE FOR SIN AND ADDICTIONS

A bottle of grace and solutions for persistent sin and addictions

All scriptures in this bottle are taken from the King James Version of the Bible unless otherwise indicated.

The other translations used in this edition:
NKJV - NEW KING JAMES VERSION
NIV   - NEW INTERNATIONAL VERSION
BBE   - BIBLE IN BASIC ENGLISH
NLT   - NEW LIVING TRANSLATION
AMP   - AMPLIFIED BIBLE

God's Medicine Bottle for Sin and Addictions

Musa George Mwanza
P. O box 1015
Jeffrey's bay
6330
South Africa.

E-mail: medicine bottle @gmail .com

Cover photo: Brandon Jones

Dedication

with a heart that yearns for the salvation and the freedom of the creation of the our God the father of our Lord Jesus Christ, and with much love, prayer and a thankful heart I dedicate this bottle to the thousands will find Christ and to those who are destined to find salvation and freedom from sinful addictions through this tool. By the grace of our Lord Jesus Christ I commit you to freedom.

3

<u>Thanksgiving</u>

My thanks first and foremost go to God the father of our Lord Jesus Christ for birthing this concept of the grace bottle in me.

Secondly: to my family, my wife and children for their sacrifice. But especially, to my wife Hope for her support and contribution towards the bottle, thirdly to my LXP family, for their moral support.

PERSONAL INFORMATION

Name:

....

Home address:

....

....

Home telephone:

....

Mobil:

....

E-mail address:

....

Areas of struggle:

....

....

Resolutions:

....

....

....

Prescription

For this medicine bottle to have maximum results for you there is need for you to follow all the instructions given in this prescription. There is a specific prescribed way in which everything needs to be done to achieve maximum results.

The prescription will give you maximum information on the importance of each activity to be undertaken. The way they are to be undertaken, the times and also the frequency of doing these activities.

Below are the prescribed activities and their respective significance:

Grace pills:

Grace pills are grace articles prepared to give you an understanding of the heart of God concerning your probable situation. These grace pills are there to show you that God loves you and has provided everything you need to live a life free from sin and addictions.

These are pills that are given to treat the mind from the sickness of misconceptions about God and how He looks at you. These pills will also give you an introduction to the heart of the grace of our Lord Jesus. This grace is the abundant kindness of God to forgive sin and empower us to have dominion over sin.

Lastly the grace pills will bring to your understanding the truth that the Lord Jesus Christ did not come to condemn you for your sinful habits and addictions, but He came to save you from that sin and addictions that griped your life.

There are 10 grace pills in this bottle. Each grace pill needs to be studied diligently and meditated upon 3 times a day in times between 09:00am to 10:00am; 12:00noon to 1:00pm; 3:00pm to 4:00pm.

Study the grace pill for the day and answer the question when there is need or write down your understanding and put it to work in your life.

The grace pills shall only come up once in every three days. For example if day 1 has a grace pill, and then day 2 and day 3 will not have a grace pill. i.e.

Day	Activity	Frequency
1	Grace Pill	3 times/day
2	N/A	N/A
3	N/A	N/A
4	Grace Pill	3 times/day

Confessional prayers:

There are three confessional prayers that need to be done in the period of the therapy.

These confessional prayers are:
- ✓ Prayer for purification
- ✓ Prayer for wisdom to walk right.
- ✓ Prayer for strength in the inner man.

These prayers must be confessed by the person undertaking the therapy audibly into his/ her ears. They are meant to renew your mind and build your faith in the Word, as faith comes by hearing.

In the book of Hebrew 3:1 apostle Paul calls the Lord Jesus, the High Priest of our confession. This means that in the same way that the people in the Old Testament could take their sacrifice to the High Priest, for the High Priest to present to the Lord on their behalf. We likewise present these confession prayers in the Name of Jesus; to the Lord

Jesus, who is our High Priest to delivers on our behalf to the throne of Mercy.

The Lord Jesus pleads before the heavenly father on our behalf asking for grace to purify us from our addictions and strength and wisdom to walk right. Heb 7:25 declares *"Wherefore he is able also to save them to the uttermost that come unto God by him, seeing he ever liveth to make intercession for them."*

These prayers must be prayed everyday 3 times a day for 30days. The confessional prayers shall be shared in the 3 hours reserved for each day with grace pills and devotionals respectively.

On days when there are grace pills, they will be shared with grace pills and on days when there are devotionals, they will be shared with devotionals.

10

These prayers shall be confessed meditatively 3 times a day between the following times: 09:00am to 10:00am; 12:00noon to1:00pm; 3:00pm to 4:00pm.

The order of the 3 confessional prayers shall be as follows:

- ✓ Prayer for purification shall be from day 1 to day 10.

- ✓ Prayer for wisdom to live right shall be from day 11 to day 20.

- ✓ Prayer for strength in the inner man shall be from day 21 to day 30.

Devotionals
(For studying & meditation):

These devotionals are passages of scripture from the Word of God. In John 1: 4 the scriptures declare *"In Him (the Word) was life, and the life was the light of men."*

The light that we need to expose and subsequently destroy strongholds of sin and addictions in our lives is in the Word of truth, which is the word of God.

The Word of God is alive; it has the ability to expose every area of our lives. It judges the thoughts and the intentions of the heart. It's able to penetrate even as deep as the bone marrows to destroy sin and addictions. Heb 4:12 declares *"For the word of God is quick, and powerful, and sharper than any two-edged sword, piercing even to the dividing asunder of soul and spirit, and of the joints and marrow, and is a discerner of the thoughts and intents of the heart."* The Lord again declared in Jeremiah 23:29 *"Is not my word like a fire? saith the LORD; and like a hammer that breaketh the rock in pieces?"*

The Word of God is a fire that consumes sin and a hammer that breaks the rock of addictions into pieces in our lives. Go for the Word with all your heart and you will find freedom from the worst addiction imaginable.

The Lord Jesus prayed to the father for His disciples and asked Him to wash them from their sins and addictions with the truth, which is His Word as shown in John 17:17 *"Sanctify them through thy truth: thy word is truth."*

The Word of God is the water that washes clean, spirit, soul and body thereby purifying us from the sickness of sin. *"Now ye are clean through the word which I have spoken unto you."* (John 15:3).

Deep yourself in the Word through studying and meditating, continue doing so diligently and you'll find your freedom and growth. *"Then Jesus said to those Jews who believed Him, "If you abide (live) in My word, you are My disciples indeed. And you shall know the truth, and the truth shall make you free."* (John 8:31-32).

Abiding, living and dwelling in the Word of God makes us free from any bondage that can hold us back. Other versions of the Bible use the word "continue" to mean if we continue studying and meditating on the Word, then shall the truth manifest in us and set us free from sin and addictions.

The psalmist in Psalms 119: 105 declared *"Your word is a lamp to my feet, And the light to my path."* The Word is the light that shines in our areas of darkness. As we diligently study and meditate on the devotionals, the light of the Word will start shining our path, lighting areas of darkness in our lives thereby enabling us to walk right and in the light.

The study and meditation of the devotionals shall be done 3 times a day

14

between 09:00am to 10:00am; 12:00noon to 1:00pm; 3:00pm to 4:00pm; as shown below:

Day	Activity	Frequency
1	Grace Pill & prayer	3 times/day
2	Devotional & prayer	3 times/day
3	Devotional & prayer	3 times/day
4	Grace Pill & prayer	3 times/day

How to meditate on the Word

"This book of the law shall not depart from your mouth, but you shall <u>meditate</u> in it day and night, that you may observe to do according to all that is written in it. For then you will make your way prosperous, and then you will have good success."

(Joshua 1:8).

15

The word meditate as highlighted in the above scripture comes from a Hebrew word "HAGAH". This word "Hagah" implies to study; ponder; imagine; mutter; utter; speak and talk.

Going by the implied meaning of the word Hagah rather than the literal meaning in English language gives us a more detailed account of the practice of meditation as an art as follows.

Study:

To study is to diligently analyse something. So you have to steadily analyse the Word of God, not to be in a hurry when studying the scripture. Many believers are in the habit of just going through the scriptures, casually reading.

This is not right; it is a disservice to you as the reader. This is because you will become familiar with scripture and thereby will not get the maximum benefit from it.

The Word of God is a treasure, to one it is a source of encouragement and yet to another it is a source of power. It's up to the reader whether you casually read through and get encouraged or study diligently and get power to overcome every circumstance along your way.

Ponder:

To ponder is to dwell on the Word. This implies dissecting the Word with the aim of getting understanding and revelation behind it. You may need to go through the same passage of scripture several times and use different translations of the bible to get the mind of God and not just the written Word.

You do not have to know everything in the scriptures, but make sure the little you know is working in you. You may even study just a chapter or a few verses at a time, but make sure you get the truth out of that passage of scripture. The Bible says that if you continue in the Word you shall know the truth. *"Then said Jesus to those Jews which believed on him, If ye continue in my word, then are ye my disciples indeed; And ye shall know the truth, and the truth shall make you free."* (John 8:31).

This might mean going to the original languages the scriptures were written in like Hebrew and Greek to get the exact wording used.

Imagine:

To imagine is to make a mental picture of the Word. Christ Jesus is the manifested Word of God in to flesh. So you should know what the Word of God at work looks like, it looks like the person and life of Jesus Christ.

When for instance you study a passage of scripture which talks about how the Lord Jesus healed someone of disease and sickness. Make a picture in your mind of how He did it.

Because that's the same way the Word will do it for you if you have faith in it. The more time you spend thinking and imaging something, the more you become like it and the more you fall in love with it.

Therefore if you spend more time thinking, imagining and picturing on the Word of God and how it worked in the life and earthly ministry of our Lord Jesus. It will start working the same way in you and the more your life become like Jesus and the more you fall in love with the idea of the Word of God working the same way in your life and ministry.

Mutter:

To mutter is to speak under your breath. After you have a mental picture of the Word of God at work, you get some understanding and enlightenment and so you start to speak the Word under your breath.

You continue muttering the Word until the authority of the Word of God starts to take over you. The more you mutter the Word, the more you fill your heart warming up with the power of the Word.

This will give you unusual energy, and you will unconsciously start rising your voice and before you know it, you will be filled with joy and peace.

Utter:

To utter is to speak with an audible voice. As your voice starts rising from muttering the Word, you automatically get into uttering the Word with a loud voice into your heart through your ears.

This process will convert your heart and change the course of your life. The more you utter the Word in to your ears the more it changes you. The Word is a seed of transformation that gets planted straight into the fertile ground of your heart.

This process deals with speaking the exact Word of God into your ears and heart; this is the Logos, the written Word of God. When the Word sinks into your heart, it will cause you to speak words for your exact situation.

Speak:

To speak is to talk with insight. After the Word fills your heart, your heart will start channeling the course of your life in the ways of the Word of God. *"A man's heart deviseth his ways."* (Psalms 16:9). It will cause you to start speaking to and about yourself in line with the Word of God. *"......for out of the abundance of the heart the mouth speaketh."* (Mathew12:34).

Rhema will start coming out of your mouth. Rhema is the living word coming from a heart that is filled with the Word of God. This is the now word you speak concerning your situation. It is a word like *"I am not condemned!" "Christ became sin and destroyed the power of sin and addictions through his death!" "Therefore this sin has no dominion over me!" "it has no authority over my life!"*

The son has set me free from every sin and addiction and therefore I am free from this addiction.

Talk:

To talk is to discuss with another. This Word therefore propels us to share our revelations with our friends. The more we share what the Lord has done or is doing in our lives, the more we overcome. Revelations 12:11 declares that they overcome the enemy by the word of their testimonies.

The sin and addictions is your enemy, so don't be afraid to testify in faith about what the Lord has accomplished for you on the cross.

Fasting days:

Every Wednesdays and Fridays of the 30 days are to be consecrated for fasting days. The purpose of this fast is to weaken the flesh and it's cravings as we work to overcome the addictions.

Sinful lusts and addictions are strengthened by the power of the flesh. Therefore when we fast we weaken the resolve of the flesh and thereby giving the Spirit of the Lord power to work in us and deliver us from the addictions and sinful lusts. *"For the flesh lusts against the Spirit, and the Spirit against the flesh; and these are contrary to one another, that you may not do the things that you desire."*
(Galatians 5:17 WEB).

The period of each particular fast shall be between Tuesdays midnight to Wednesday 4:00pm the following day and Thursday's midnight to Friday 4:00pm the following day. This shall be a total fast, meaning there shall be No liquids and No solids. Breaking of the fast must occur Wednesdays and Fridays after the evening sacrifice of 3:00pm to 4:00pm.

Why the three periods of prayer?

The three times are the times for daily sacrifice. During these times I believe heaven is open to receive our daily sacrifices.

As we do this exercise we present our bodies as living sacrifices three times a day, thereby declaring our inadequacy in dealing with our addictions.

This is the wisdom that the prophets of old used to access heaven and we choose to use the same wisdom.

Three hours are to be set apart daily for this sacrifice, between the following times;

09:00am to 10:00am   Morning sacrifice
12:00noon to 1:00pm   Noon sacrifice
03:00pm to 4:00pm   Evening sacrifice.

NOTE: this is not law, so if these time periods will not work for you. Then you can find the 3 hours in a day that you can dedicate to the work of the Lord in your life.

Addictions that result from curses and involvements in occult and satanic practices:

There are addictions and sins which run in family bloodlines, from generation to generation. For instance the struggles in sin and addictions that your grandparents passed through are brought down to you, from your parents and perhaps are further passed down to your children.

Such kinds of sin and addictions run in the family bloodline, and are mostly caused and enforced by curses. There are certain practices of sin which provoke curses; for instance the sin of homosexuality, the sin of immorality and the sin of witchcraft.

If you involved yourself in such vices, you provoked curses which will run in your family bloodline to the third and forth generations if not broken along the way.

Many families are arrested in sin and addictions by the devil using the power of such curses. These curses empower a certain evil practice in the family. Practices such as smoking, drug abuse, alcohol abuse, witchcraft and immorality etc.

These addictions are driven and cemented in people's lives by the curse that runs in the family. The curse becomes the engine that empowers certain practices making the family vulnerable to the sin and addiction.

Unless this curse is broken it will continue running in the family repeating the same addictions and sins as in generations passed.

Many families have resigned to accepting certain practices as family weaknesses, because they have noticed the recurring nature of the addiction and sin in the family. They have tried and failed to stop the habit in the family line and now have accepted it as a family weakness.

It is not the will of God for any family to have an evil weakness; it all comes from the enemy the devil.

Other areas responsible for family bondages and addictive sin are the involvements in ancestral worship, occultism, witchcraft and Satanism. These involvements invoke demon spirits which invite a lot of curses upon a person's life. It is curses from such practices that invite addictions such as spiritual impurity, immorality, drug abuse and excessive alcohol abuse in families, dullness of perception.

Curses which prevent anybody from becoming something in the families, for instance nobody has ever done university or college education in the family. Every one ends up in the same place as their parents, no progress registered over the generations.

These addictions are caused and effected by the evil spirits that enter our lives and families through such involvements as mentioned above. Many of our African brothers and sisters are victims of these curses. This is because of our cultural deep rooted, involvements with the evil spirits, through worshipping of ancestral spirits and other gods.

These practices are responsible for the shallow mindedness of most of our African people, the poverty and excessive drinking of alcohol and many other vices.

In many of our cultures blood sacrifice is very common to appease the spirits of our ancestors and other gods. But one thing we are blinded on is the truth that blood sacrifice opens our lives to the spiritual world.

These doors can lead to the Holy Spirit through the blood sacrifice of Christ Jesus which results into blessings or to the demon spirits through the goats and other animal sacrifice to the gods and ancestors unto curses and sinful addictions.

Now since these curses and there effects thereof run in the family bloodline, they will affect everyone born in the family to the third and fourth generation if not broken. This amounts to between 120 to 160 years from provocation, meaning anyone born in that family line in this period of time will be affected by the curse resulting into addictions, limitations and many other vices.

If you identify with any of these involvements as mentioned above, whether at family or personal level, you need to follow the 7 steps process to release as listed below to help you get out of the snare of the enemy.

1. Confess your faith in Christ and His sacrifice on your behalf.

The scripture in Romans 10:9-10 gives us two essential conditions for receiving the benefits of Christ's sacrifice for us;

- ✓ To believe in your heart that God raised Jesus from the dead.
- ✓ To confess with your mouth that Jesus is Lord over your life.

Now faith in your heart is not fully effective until it has been completed by confession with your mouth. So you need to confess with your mouth as follows; (Confess out loud)

```
I believe in my heart, that
Jesus died for my sins on the
cross of Calvary, and God raised
Him from the dead on the third
day for my justification. And
now I confess with my mouth that
the Lord Jesus is Lord over my
life to the praise of his glory.
```

2. Repent of all your rebellion and sin.

First of all you must take personal responsibility for your rebellious attitude towards God and for the sin that resulted from it. Here is a suggested confession that expresses the repentance that God demands:

(Confess out loud)

```
I   acknowledge   my   rebellious
attitude  towards  you  my  God;  I
choose   to   give   up   all   my
rebellion  and  all  my  sins.  I
submit   myself   (mind,   will   &
heart)  to  you  as  my  Lord.
```

3. Receive forgiveness of all sin.

The great barrier that keeps God's freedom out of our lives is unforgiven sin. God has already made grace available for all of our sins to be forgiven, but He will not do it until we confess them. It might be that God has shown you certain sins that opened you up to a curse. If so make a specific confession of those sins.

Take time to look into your life, and think through very carefully and then ask God to show you if there is any hidden sin in your life that needs to be confessed. *"If we confess our sins, He is faithful and just to forgive us our sins and to cleanse us from all unrighteousness."* (1John 1:9).

4. Forgive all other people who have ever harmed you or wronged you.

Another great barrier that can keep God's freedom out of our lives is unforgiveness in our hearts towards other people. Forgiving another person is not primarily an emotion; but a decision. Ask God to bring to your mind anyone you need to forgive.

The Holy Spirit will prompt you to make the right decision, but He will not make it for you. Here is a suggestion on how to forgive others;

```
Say  it  loud,  "Lord,  I  forgive
(name  them) ............." and  so  on  until
```

you have forgiven everyone you
need to forgive.

5. Renounce all contacts with occult and satanic activities or things.

This includes a very wide range of activities and practices. If you have been involved at any time in such activities and practices, you have crossed the invisible borderline into the kingdom of Satan.

Since that time whether you know it or not, Satan has regarded you as one of his subjects. He considers that he has a legal claim to you.
You need to forever cut off all connections with Satan.

If you are unsure about any particular activity, ask God to make it clear to you. Some examples of satanic practices include witchcraft, consulting witchdoctors, fortune-tellers, divinations and many other forms of satanic worship through ancestral worship.

If you have any objects that you got from satanic sources you need to destroy such objects. These objects include all satanic and occult images, good luck charms, other charms, books and satanic alters. If there are rituals that you perform you need to stop them and renounce them.

Here is a suggestion on how to renounce such practices;
Say it loud, "Lord, I renounce (list the objects and rituals)........." and so on until you have renounced everything. Do all in the name of Jesus.

After this you need to destroy any satanic objects by burning.

6. You are now ready to pray the prayer of release from any curse.

It's important that you base your faith solely upon what Jesus obtained for you through His sacrifice on the cross. You do not have to "earn" your release, you do not have to be "worthy of it."

Prayer of release:

Lord Jesus Christ, I believe that you are the son of God and the only way to God; and that you died on the cross for my sins and rose again from the dead. I give up all my rebellion and all my sin and I submit myself to you as my Lord. I confess all my sins before you and ask you for your forgiveness--especially for any sins that exposed me to a curse.

Release me also from the consequences of my ancestors' sins. By a decision of my will, I forgive all who have harmed or wronged me--just as you have forgiven my sins. In particular, I forgive--(names). I renounce all contacts with anything satanic and occult rituals--if I have any "contact objects" I commit myself to destroy them. I cancel all Satan's claims against me. Lord Jesus, I believe that on the cross You took on yourself every curse that could ever come upon me. So I ask You now to release me from every curse over my life--in your Name, Lord Jesus Christ I pray.

By faith I now receive my release from every curse that causes sinful addictions and I

give You thanks Dear Lord Jesus
for releasing me in your Name;
Jesus Christ I pray, full of
thanksgiving in my heart AMEN!

7. Now believe that you have received God's freedom and act that way.

At this stage you need to give thanks to the Lord for He has given you freedom from the curse that kept you in bondage of sin. You may still feel the same symptoms but never mind just testify about His goodness and give Him praise because the curse that empowered the addiction has been broken over your life. There may be a manifestation of the spirit empowering the curse or not, but do not but moved if there is none. All the same spirit that empowered the curse is gone.

From this point on you are free from the curse that enforced the addiction, but you still need to go through the next stages of the therapy. This is in order to give you understanding of how Christ looks at you and to break those sinful habits that formed in you as a result of the curse that worked in you.

Day One

Grace pill no. 1

We all belong.

"The earth is the Lord's, with all its wealth; the world and all the people living in it."
(Psalms 24:1 BBE).

*W*e all belong somewhere; both you and I belong to a family, a social class, a city, a nation, a continent and a racial grouping and many more. We all belong somewhere, that's why we have different surnames to show that we belong to different clans and genealogies.

The different identities we posses have a direct impact on our value systems and therefore controls the way we look at things.

The above opening scripture declares that the earth and all its wealth belongs to the Lord, the world and all the people that exist in it belong to the Lord. This means that if you live in this world then you belong to the world and the world belongs to the Lord.

Mother earth also belongs to a group of planets in the universe. And all the planets in the heavens belong to the Lord. This therefore means that all the treasure and people of this creation belong to the Lord God of Heaven. Deuteronomy 10:14 declares *"Behold, the heaven and the heaven of heavens is the LORD'S thy God, the earth also, with all that therein is."* All the galaxies in the heavens are the Lord's, you and I inclusive.

The Psalmist declared in Psalms 115:16 that *"The heaven, even the heavens, are the LORD'S: but the earth hath he given to the children of men."* The Lord gave us the earth to live in, but He owns everything and everyone. This is the reason why even the heavens declare the glory of God; And the firmament show His handiwork. **(Psalms 19:1).** Both we; the heavens and the earth and its inhabitant were created to show forth His glory.

We all were created; we all come from somewhere. Children come from the union between man and woman, and all other things come from the earth. Just like we prepare for the birth of children and make the house so habitable for them. He who made the earth also made it so habitable for mankind, because we are His children, His creation and He loved us even before He created us and had goodwill towards us.

John the revelator declared by the spirit that He created us by His will. You are not an accident you were created by His choice. *"You are worthy, O Lord to receive glory and honour and power; for you created all things, and by your will they exist and were created."* (Revelations 4:11).

We were created by a supreme, loving and sovereign being, who created us for Himself. We all belong to Him and not to ourselves. Therefore if and when we live for ourselves, according to our own instincts and desires we rebel against our creator. The God, who loved us, created us according to His will and gave us mother earth, with all its treasure and good things to enjoy.

Now every person was made to submit to some authority and acknowledge ruler ship over their lives. As for you:

Who do you acknowledge as your master?

- Is it circumstances; is it money or ways of the world, like drunkardness, cigarette, and sex?

Who do you obey?
Whose voice is law to your heart?

- Is it the Lord Jesus? Is it your Friends? Is it your family? Or maybe is it Satan?

Who do you put your life in? Who do you trust your life with?

- Is it the Lord Jesus? Is it your mother or father? Is it your friends? Is it life assurance policy? Is it Doctor Genius? Is it shares in Johannesburg stock exchange?

Who has dominion over your life?

- Is it your stomach? Is it your desires for more? Is it God your creator? Or maybe is it the devil, the destroyer of the earth and all who live in it?

Who are you?

To whom do you belong?

Prayer for purification

Who can discern his errors?
But your word Oh Lord, which is
living and power, and is sharper
than any two edged sword, it
pierces even to the dividing of
soul and spirit, and of joints
and marrow, and your Word is the
discerner of the thoughts and
intentions of the heart.
Cleanse me Oh Lord from my
secret faults, by your truth;
your Word is truth.
Keep back your servant also from
willful and addictive sins by
your word; for your Word is a
fire that burns the sin in the
heart from the root and the
hammer that breaks the rocks of

addictions into pieces. Then
these willful sins and
addictions will not have
dominion over me and I will be
blameless and innocent from the
great trespass.

Wash me thoroughly from my sins
and cleanse me from my addiction
by your Word.

Create in me a clean heart and
renew a steadfast spirit within
me. Restore to me the joy of your
salvation and uphold me by your
generous spirit.

And finally dear Lord may the
words of my mouth and the
meditation of my heart be
acceptable in your sight. IN THE
NAME OF JESUS CHRIST I PRAY AMEN.

Day Two

Devotions for the day;

Morning sacrifice

Between   09:00hours to 10:00hours

Passage   Psalms 119:1 to 8; plus
                Purification prayer

Noon sacrifice

Between   12:00hours to 13:00hours pm

Passage   Psalms 119: 9 to 16; plus
                Purification prayer

Evening sacrifice

Between   15:00hours to 16:00hours

Passage   Psalms 119:17 to 24; plus
                Purification prayer

Note: you should share the hour between the activities above according as you feel lead and if these times won't work for you please pick three separate hours of your own.

Day Three

Devotions for the day;

Morning sacrifice

Between   09:00hours to 10:00hours

Passage   Psalms 119:25 to 32; plus
           Purification prayer

Noon sacrifice

Between   12:00hours to 13:00hours pm

Passage   Psalms 119: 33 to 40; plus
           Purification prayer

Evening sacrifice

Between   15:00hours to 16:00hours

Passage   Psalms 119:41 to 48; plus
           Purification prayer

Note: you should share the hour between the activities above according as you feel lead and if these times won't work for you please pick three separate hours of your own.

Day Four

Grace pill no.2

All men are conceived and born in sin.

> *"Surely I was sinful at birth, sinful from the time my mother conceived me."*
> *(Psalms 51:5 NIV).*

*M*any folks around the world have questioned the need for a saviour. Many think if they do good works like helping the needy and poor in society and if they are generally good people then they have earned their way into heaven. This is the wisdom of man at work in this ideology; we can never do good enough to earn us a place into heaven.

This wisdom is so rampant in this world such that even the Islam religion is based on the same ideology of good deeds versus bad deeds to enter heaven. This is all wrong; it's the wisdom of the world that makes saints out of people who have done many good deeds.

Today the world rewards people who have done good deeds with the Noble peace prize. These good deeds are popularly known as Humanitarian work. Apostle Paul had this to say about this kind of righteous deeds in (Romans 10:3). *"For they being ignorant of God's righteousness, and going about to establish their own righteousness, have not submitted themselves unto the righteousness of God."*

The opening scripture declares that we are all born in sin; we are sinful at birth from our mother's womb. With this in mind we should always know that we cannot do righteous deeds when we are in a state of sin.

This is because all our works originate from the heart and if our hearts are sinful, then our good works are sinful as well. These good deeds or humanitarian works are as filthy rags to God. Isaiah 64:6 declares *"But we are all as an unclean thing, and all our righteousnesses are as filthy rags; and we all do fade as a leaf; and our iniquities, like the wind, have taken us away."*

This is worldly righteousness and it will never stand up for you when it really matters. It can be your defense in this world but not in heaven. All men are born in sin and therefore have a sinful nature from birth. This means that any good deeds done in this world with this nature of sin is done in sin. *"The scriptures declare that all have sinned and fallen short of the Glory of God."* (Romans 3:23).

No man in this sinful nature can do anything that is pleasing and acceptable to God and therefore reach his Glory. We need to put to death the nature of sin in us, for us to be able to do anything that is pleasing and acceptable to the Lord.

True righteousness is the true nature of God, and a person with a sinful nature cannot do deeds which are truly righteous. We all need to die to our nature of sin and put on the nature of true righteousness. The apostle Paul in (Romans 3:22) declared that *"This righteousness from God comes through faith in Jesus Christ to all who believe."* And also in (2 Corinthians 5:17), He declares that *"Therefore, if anyone is in Christ, he is a new creation, the old (nature of sin) has gone,*

53

and the new (nature of righteousness) has come!"

We all need to acknowledge the truth that we all are born sinful in nature and there is nothing we can do in this nature to be saved from eternal damnation. We can earn our way on earth and in this world but not eternity.

We all need to believe in Christ Jesus and acknowledge Him as the Lord of our lives to be saved from eternal damnation. True righteousness is imputed into our spirit through acknowledging Christ Jesus as our Lord and saviour. *"For with the heart one believes unto righteousness..."* (Romans 10:10).

Christ took on himself the nature of sin and was punished on the cross of Calvary on behalf of sinful mankind. This was in order to punish the sinful nature once and for all so

that through Him we might be the
righteousness of God in him. (2 Corinthians
5:21).

It's only through believing in the finished
work of Christ Jesus on the cross of Calvary
that we can be truly righteous.

Prayer for purification

Who can discern his errors?
But your word Oh Lord, which is
living and power, and is sharper
than any two edged sword, it
pierces even to the dividing of
soul and spirit, and of joints
and marrow, and your word is the
discerner of the thoughts and
intentions of the heart.
Cleanse me Oh Lord from my
secret faults, by your truth;
your word is truth.
Keep back your servant also from
willful and addictive sins by

your word; for your word is a
fire that burns the sin in the
heart from the root and the
hammer that breaks the rocks of
addictions into pieces. Then
these willful sins and
addictions will not have
dominion over me and I will be
blameless and innocent from the
great trespass.
Wash me thoroughly from my sins
and cleanse me from my addiction
by your word.
Create in me a clean heart and
renew a steadfast spirit within
me. Restore to me the joy of your
salvation and uphold me by your
generous spirit.
And finally dear Lord may the
words of my mouth and the
meditation of my heart be
acceptable in your sight. IN THE
NAME OF JESUS CHRIST I PRAY AMEN.

Day Five

Devotions for the day;

Morning sacrifice

Between   09:00hours to 10:00hours

Passage   Psalms 119:49 to 56; plus
Purification prayer

Noon sacrifice

Between   12:00hours to 13:00hours pm

Passage   Psalms 119: 57 to 64; plus
Purification prayer

Evening sacrifice

Between   15:00hours to 16:00hours

Passage   Psalms 119:65 to 72; plus
Purification prayer

Note: you should share the hour between the activities above according as you feel lead and if these times won't work for you please pick three separate hours of your own.

Day Six

Devotions for the day;

Morning sacrifice

Between   09:00hours to 10:00hours

Passage   Psalms 119:73 to 80; plus
           Purification prayer

Noon sacrifice

Between   12:00hours to 13:00hours pm

Passage   Psalms 119: 81 to 88; plus
           Purification prayer

Evening sacrifice

Between   15:00hours to 16:00hours

Passage   Psalms 119:89 to 96; plus
           Purification prayer

Note: you should share the hour between the activities above according as you feel lead and if these times won't work for you please pick three separate hours of your own.

Day Seven

Grace pill no.3

You cannot clean yourself from sin.

> **Who can say, "I have made my heart clean, I am pure from my sin?"**
> *(Proverbs 20:9 NKJV).*

*M*any folks around the world are misled by the systems of this world to believe that they can cleanse themselves from sin.

Many look at sin only to be physical, earthly and not spiritual. They only care when they offend or sin against their friends and family. They have no clue that sin is firstly committed against the creator. They are so earthly minded such that they think that a compensation, or settling the matter in the courts of law is enough to cleanse them from sin.

It's wrong to think that way, no good deeds or compensation will ever separate you from your sin. No one can cleanse themselves from their sins. The Lord and father of our Lord Jesus Christ declared by his Spirit through prophet Jeremiah in chapter 2:22, saying *"for though you wash yourself with lye, and use much soap, yet your iniquity (sin) is marked before me,"* this means we cannot escape from sin cheaply.

The problem of sin is a spiritual problem and therefore always demands blood sacrifice to be removed or cleansed. Our forefathers in the Old Testament used the blood sacrifice of goats and bulls to atone for their sins, but this wasn't sufficient enough because it was not a permanent removal of sin.

The High Priest had to present a sacrifice every year for the atonement of the sins of the people with the blood of goats and bulls. This is confirmed by scriptures in Hebrews 9:7 which declares *"But into the second part (Holy of Holies) the high priest alone once a year, not without blood, which he offered for himself and for the people's sins committed in ignorance."*

Unlike the blood of goats and bulls, which could only cover and cleanse the sins for a season, the blood of Jesus Christ our saviour came to cleanse us from sin forever. Jesus unlike the high priests of old did not sin, therefore did not sacrifice for His own sins and more powerfully He did not enter into the Holy of Holies with the blood of goats and bulls but with His own blood He entered the

61

most Holy place and atoned for our sin once and for all.

He came to be the sin sacrifice for all who are born and live in this world. That's the reason why when John the Baptist saw Jesus coming in John 1:29, declared *"behold the lamb of God who takes away the sin of the world."* It's only Jesus who can take away your sin and no one else.

He was given power to take away sin because He paid for it with His own blood. The scripture in Hebrews 9:11-14 summed it up as perfectly as shown below; *"But Christ came as High Priest of the good things to come, with the greater and more perfect tabernacle not made with hands, that is not of this creation, Not with the blood of goats and calves, but with His own blood He entered the most Holy Place once for all, having obtained eternal redemption. For if the blood of bulls and goats and the ashes of a heifer, sprinkling the unclean, sanctifies for the purifying of the flesh, how much more shall the blood of Christ, who through the eternal Spirit offered Himself without spot to God, cleanse your conscience from dead works to serve the living God?"*

Give your life to Jesus and He will cleanse you from your sins, which are able to destroy your life. *"But if we walk in the light (the word) as He is in the light (the word), we have fellowship with one another, and the blood of Jesus Christ His son cleanses us from all sin."* (1 John 1:7).

If we walk in the Word of the scriptures, the blood of Jesus Christ His son cleanses us from all forms of sin and all form of addictions!

"And ye know that he was manifested to take away our sins; and in him is no sin."

(1John 3:5).

Choose life, choose freedom from sin, choose Jesus Christ as your saviour, choose the Word of God which is Christ manifested in the Word.

Prayer for purification

Who can discern his errors? But your Word Oh Lord, which is living and power, and is sharper than any two edged sword, it pierces even to the dividing of soul and spirit, and of joints and marrow, and your Word is the discerner of the thoughts and intentions of the heart.

Cleanse me Oh Lord from my secret faults, by your truth; your word is truth.

Keep back your servant also from willful and addictive sins by your word; for your word is a fire that burns the sin in the heart from the root and the hammer that breaks the rocks of addictions into pieces. Then these willful sins and addictions will not have dominion over me and I will be blameless and innocent from the great trespass.

Wash me thoroughly from my sins and cleanse me from my addiction by your Word.

Create in me a clean heart and renew a steadfast spirit within me. Restore to me the joy of your salvation and uphold me by your generous spirit.

And finally dear Lord may the words of my mouth and the meditation of my heart be acceptable in your sight. IN THE NAME OF JESUS CHRIST I PRAY AMEN.

Day Eight

Devotions for the day;

Morning sacrifice

Between   09:00hours to 10:00hours

Passage   Psalms 119:97 to 104; plus
Purification prayer

Noon sacrifice

Between   12:00hours to 13:00hours pm

Passage   Psalms 119:105 to 112; plus
Purification prayer

Evening sacrifice

Between   15:00hours to 16:00hours

Passage   Psalms 119:113 to 120; plus
Purification prayer

Note: you should share the hour between the activities above according as you feel lead and if these times won't work for you please pick three separate hours of your own.

Day Nine

Devotions for the day;

Morning sacrifice

Between   09:00hours to 10:00hours

Passage   Psalms 119:121 to 128; plus
                Purification prayer

Noon sacrifice

Between   12:00hours to 13:00hours pm

Passage   Psalms 119: 129 to 136; plus
                Purification prayer

Evening sacrifice

Between   15:00hours to 16:00hours

Passage   Psalms 119:137 to 144; plus
                Purification prayer

Note: you should share the hour between the activities above according as you feel lead and if these times won't work for you please pick three separate hours of your own.

Day Ten

Don't write yourself off because of your sinful habits.

".....But where sin is bounded, grace did much more abound."
(Romans 5:20).

*M*any people around the world have been deceived by the enemy the devil, friends and even family into believing that their situation is irreversible. Many have resigned to being sinners and addicts because of self pity and what their friends have told them concerning their situation.

Some people would even say "whoa! That sin is too big or that addiction is irreversible not even Jesus can cure that addiction or forgive that sin". Such people have managed to deliver many into the hands of the devil out of ignorance.

There are some other people who think that the sin they've committed is too terrible to be forgiven. These kinds of people perceive that particular sin as unforgivable, because they probably couldn't reverse the consequences.

Such people remain in condemnation for the rest of their lives, because they think that no one can forgive them of this sin. If you are in this place of condemnation, I have good news for you; Jesus came to pay for that particular sin you're struggling with. He does not condemn you, but He is reaching out to you, to save you from the sin and condemnation that torments you.

Therefore don't judge and condemn yourself because Jesus came not to judge, nor to condemn you but to save from your distress. The scripture in John 3:17 declare *"For God sent not his Son into the world to condemn the world; but that the world through him might be saved."*

> *"And if any man hear my words, and believe not, I judge him not: for I came not to judge the world, but to save the world."* (John 12:47).

Do not focus on the sin you committed but focus on the saviour and the price He paid for your sins. If you accept Jesus as your Lord and saviour, you automatically accept the full price for the sin you committed and therefore become justified.

If you are justified you are proven innocent of the sin because somebody has paid the full price for the offence.

> *"Therefore being justified by faith, we have peace with God through our Lord Jesus Christ."* (Romans 5:1).

Another trap that the enemy uses to keep people in sin is the lie of sinning against the Holy Spirit. Many are bound in condemnation because they think that they have sinned against the Holy Spirit.

All these are lies from the pit of hell; the person who can sin against the Holy Spirit must first satisfy the conditions of Hebrews 6:4 -5. This declares:

"For it is impossible for those who were once enlightened, and have tasted of the heavenly gift, and were made partakers of the Holy Ghost, and have tasted the good Word of God, and the powers of the world to come."

A summary of the conditions are as follows:

- ✓ Once enlightened_ meaning you once had a deep understanding of the mysteries of the wisdom of God.
- ✓ Have tasted the Heavenly gifts_ meaning you once functioned in the heavenly gifts like the gift of healing.

- ✓ Have become partakers of the Holy Spirit _ meaning you once have been baptized in the Holy

Spirit with the evidence of speaking in tongues.

✓ Have tasted the good Word of God_ meaning you once understood the power and authority of the Word of God and have experienced it.

✓ Tasted the powers of the age to come _ meaning you once had a deep understanding of the supernatural power of God and have experienced it.

If you once had a good understanding and you've functioned in the above mentioned, then can you be a candidate of sinning against the Holy Spirit.

The opening scripture quoted in the New Living Translation brings more clarity to this truth …..It reads in part *"God's law was given so that all people could see how sinful they were. But as people sinned more and more, God's wonderful kindness (grace) became more abundant."*

This brothers and sisters shows us that the more sin we committed, the greater the kindness of God towards us. This therefore means that there is no amount of sin that is outside the abundant kindness of God who is Jesus Christ our Lord.

Don't think you are irreversible or the sin you committed is outside the price Christ paid for with His blood. 2 Corinthians 5:21 declares that Jesus Christ become sin itself, so that He can be punished for any and every kind of sin that could ever be committed on earth.

John the Baptist, when he saw Jesus coming in John 1:29 declared *"Behold the lamb of God who takes away the <u>sin</u> of the world."* John the Baptist did not say SINS OF

THE WORLD, to symbolize the particular types of sins. But he said SIN OF THE WORLD, to symbolize the whole disease called sin.

Jesus Christ paid for every sin imaginable, every addiction imaginable and made you free on the cross some 2000 years ago. All you need to do is to accept Him as your personal Lord and saviour, and study His Word, which is truth and it, shall set you free from your sin and addictions.

> *"And ye shall know the truth,*
> *and the truth shall make you*
> *free."*   (John 8:32).

Give Christ a chance to deliver you from your sins and bondage into a life of joy and freedom. Give Him your life and He will give you His, which is full of righteousness, peace and joy.

Go ahead; take a step by following the prayer in the next page.

Prayer of salvation:

Dear Lord Jesus I believe that you came and died for my sins on the cross; I believe that you died on the cross for my sins and were raised from the dead for my justification; I declare you Lord over my life and confess you to be my saviour; I believe the old nature of sin is gone and the new nature of righteousness has come, which is from God; I believe am born again; I thank you Jesus for giving me eternal life; I thank you righteous father for making me your righteousness in Christ Jesus AMEN!

Prayer for purification

Who can discern his errors?
But your word Oh Lord, which is
living and power, and is sharper
than any two edged sword, it
pierces even to the dividing of
soul and spirit, and of joints
and marrow, and your Word is the
discerner of the thoughts and
intentions of the heart.
Cleanse me Oh Lord from my
secret faults, by your truth;
your word is truth.
Keep back your servant also from
willful and addictive sins by
your word; for your Word is a
fire that burns the sin in the
heart from the root and the
hammer that breaks the rocks of
addictions into pieces. Then
these willful sins and
addictions will not have
dominion over me and I will be

blameless and innocent from the great trespass.

Wash me thoroughly from my sins and cleanse me from my addiction by your word.

Create in me a clean heart and renew a steadfast spirit within me. Restore to me the joy of your salvation and uphold me by your generous spirit.

And finally dear Lord may the words of my mouth and the meditation of my heart be acceptable in your sight. IN THE NAME OF JESUS CHRIST I PRAY AMEN.

Day Eleven

Devotions for the day;

Morning sacrifice
Between   09:00hours to 10:00hours

Passage   Psalms 119:145 to 152; plus
           Purification prayer

Noon sacrifice
Between   12:00hours to 13:00hours pm

Passage   Psalms 119: 153 to 160; plus
           Purification prayer

Evening sacrifice
Between   15:00hours to 16:00hours

Passage   Psalms 119:161 to 168; plus
           Purification prayer

Note: you should share the hour between the activities above according as you feel lead and if these times won't work for you please pick three separate hours of your own.

Day Twelve

Devotions for the day;

Morning sacrifice

Between   09:00hours to 10:00hours

Passage   Psalms 119:169 to 176; plus
           Purification prayer

Noon sacrifice

Between   12:00hours to 13:00hours pm

Passage   Psalms 120: 1 to 8; plus
           Purification prayer

Evening sacrifice

Between   15:00hours to 16:00hours

Passage   Psalms 121:1 to 8; plus
           Purification prayer

Note: you should share the hour between the activities above according as you feel lead and if these times won't work for you please pick three separate hours of your own.

Day Thirteen

Grace pill no.5

Jesus paid the full price for every sin.

"God made him who had no sin to be sin for us, so that in Him we might become the righteousness of God."
(2 Corinthians 5:21 NIV).

*T*he opening scripture gives us a picture of how Jesus was made sin with our sinfulness, so that in Him we might be the righteousness of God. Jesus who had committed no sin was made the worst sinner that can ever be in this world, so that He can deliver any and every kind of sinner into the righteousness of God.

82

The God of heaven made Jesus His precious son a scapegoat for our sins, He rejected Him with our rejection, the rejection that was meant for a sinner like you and me so that in Him we might find acceptance with God the father.

Jesus paid the full price for our sins; He was made the High Priest of our souls and paid for our sins through suffering. The Spirit of the Lord through prophet Isaiah in the book of Isaiah 53:1-10 said this about our High Priest; *"Who has believed our report? And to whom has the arm of the Lord been revealed? For He shall grow up before Him as a tender plant, And as a root out of dry ground. He has no form or comeliness; And when we see Him, There is no beauty that we should desire Him, He is despised and rejected by men, A man of sorrows and acquainted with grief. And we hid, as it*

83

were, our faces from Him; He was despised, and we did not esteem Him. Surely He has borne our griefs and carried our sorrows; Yet we esteemed Him stricken, smitten by God, and afflicted. But He was wounded for our transgressions (sins), He was bruised for our iniquities; The chastisement(punishment) for our peace was upon Him, And by His stripes we are healed. All we like sheep have gone astray; We have turned, every one, to his own way; And the Lord has laid on Him the iniquity (sin) of us all. He was oppressed and He was afflicted, Yet He opened not His mouth; He was led as a lamb to the slaughter, And as a sheep before the shearer is silent, so He opened not His mouth. He was taken from prison and from judgment, And who will declare His generation? For He was cut off from the land of the living; For the transgressions (sins) of my people He was stricken. And they made His grave with the wicked- But with the rich at His death, Because He had done no violence, Nor was any deceit in His mouth. Yet it pleased the Lord to bruise Him; He has put Him to grief. When You make His soul an offering (sacrifice) for sin, He shall see His seed, He shall prolong His days, And the pleasure of the Lord shall prosper in His hand."

What manner of man is this?
A man who willingly suffered and paid the price for the sin He did not commit?

The above scripture declares in detail, what the man Jesus had to go through for our sins. He suffered the worst form of humiliation, pain and even death for you and me. For a people who do not care; a people who do not want to not change; a people who love sin.

"And this is love, not that we had love for God, but that he had love for us, and sent his Son to be an offering (payment) for our sins." (1John 4:10 BBE).

Christ was moved by His love for us, to take our place of sin and suffer the consequences thereof that you and I may escape death that comes from sin and the judgment that comes thereafter.

"But God commendeth his love toward us, in that, while we were yet sinners, Christ died for us." (Romans 5:8).

He did not consider how much we loved sinning nor how much we did not want to repent but because He loved us so much, He came and paid the full price for our sins with His own life through His death on the cross.

Do not continue to live in sin because Jesus loves you so much, He already paid the full price for your sin. Just make up your mind and walk away from sin without shame or condemnation. Jesus loves you so much and He will take away your sin as far as the east is from the west if you come to Him in repentance.

God the father of our Lord Jesus Christ did all this in order to present for Himself a righteous generation in Christ, a people who are called by His Name.

Therefore if you confess Jesus to be your Lord and saviour and believe in your heart that He paid the whole price of sin for you, you shall be saved and qualify to be the righteousness of God in Christ.

Prayer for wisdom to walk right

God of my Lord Jesus Christ,
merciful Lord, by your Word, you
created everything. By your
wisdom you made man to rule over
all creation, to govern the
world with holiness and
righteousness, to administer
justice with integrity.
Give me the wisdom that sits
besides your throne; give me a
place among those who are
sanctified.
I am your servant and I am only
human, I am not strong and my
life will be short without your
Word. I have little
understanding of your Word or
how to apply it.
Even if a man is perfect in his
ways, he will be thought of as
nothing without the wisdom that
comes from you.

You chose to die for me, on the cross so that I may know your ways. Wisdom is with you and knows your ways; she was present when you made the world. She knows what pleases you; what is right and in accordance to your commands.

Send her from your holy heavens, down from your glorious throne, so that she may work in my heart, and I may learn what pleases you.

She knows and understands everything, and will guide wisely in everything I do. Her glory will protect me and I will walk wisely in everything I do; then will my ways and deeds be acceptable unto you. IN THE NAME OF JESUS CHRIST I PRAY AMEN.

Day Fourteen

Devotions for the day;

Morning sacrifice

Between   09:00hours to 10:00hours

Passage   Psalms 126:1 to 6; plus prayer for
Wisdom

Noon sacrifice

Between   12:00hours to 13:00hours pm

Passage   Psalms 125: 1 to 5; plus prayer for
Wisdom

Evening sacrifice

Between   15:00hours to 16:00hours

Passage   Psalms 129:1 to 8; plus prayer for s
Wisdom

Note: you should share the hour between the activities above according as you feel lead and if these times won't work for you please pick three separate hours of your own.

Day Fifteen

Devotions for the day;

Morning sacrifice

Between   09:00hours to 10:00hours

Passage   Psalms 23:1 to 6; plus prayer for
Wisdom

Noon sacrifice

Between   12:00hours to 13:00hours pm

Passage   Psalms 18: 1 to 8; plus prayer for
Wisdom

Evening sacrifice

Between   15:00hours to 16:00hours

Passage   Psalms 18:9 to 15; plus prayer for
Wisdom

Note: you should share the hour between the activities above according as you feel lead and if these times won't work for you please pick three separate hours of your own.

Day sixteen

Grace pill no.6

You are the image of God.

"So God created man in his own image, In the image of God he created him male and female he created them."

(Genesis 1:27 NIV).

*M*an is the crown of the creation of God. He is the finest of all of God's creation and the reason for creating everything that is good and pleasant on earth. Man is the reason why God the father created everything good on earth because the He wanted to first and foremost create a place for man to stay.

When God was creating everything else, He didn't say *"in our image let us create plants or animals."* He created everything else according to their respective kind and not according his image and likeness. But when it came to man, God pause and said let us create man according to our image and in our likeness. Take very good look at Genesis 1:26 to see the picture of you in the eyes of God.

HIS IMAGE:

You are the most beautiful of all of His creations. You were made with caution, nothing about you was made in a hurry, and it was fearfully and wonderfully put together by the hands of the highest God.

The psalmist understood this truth very well such that he went about declaring that he was fearfully and wonderfully made as shown in the scripture below.

"I will praise thee; for I am fearfully and wonderfully made: marvellous are thy works; and that my soul knoweth right well." (Psalms 139:14).

Like the psalmist you must know that God the father did a marvelous work on you, He made a replica of Himself in you.

He gave man the use of five of His operations, and in the sixth place He imparted you with understanding and in the seventh speech, an interpreter of the heart and mind. He gave you a conscience; a tongue; eyes; ears and a heart. In the book of Colossians, the scripture declares that the full extent of God; the father, the son and the Holy Spirit, lived in the bodily form in Jesus.

94

**"For in him dwelleth all the
fulness of the Godhead bodily."**
(Colossians 2:9).

This means that the way Jesus was here on earth is how God the father is, with hands, with a conscience, with a tongue, eyes, ears and a heart. The way Jesus was bodily is the way we are bodily, so we possess the same features with the father, the son and the Holy Spirit. We are His reflection and all the bodily features we posses are given from Him.

*"Who is the image of the
invisible God, the firstborn
of every creature."*
(Colossians 1:15).

The Lord Jesus was the visible image of the invisible God. The way God the father is, in the invisible world, Jesus was in the visible world. He created us like Himself so that we

can be able to understand His creation and
behold his glory.

HIS LIKENESS:

The same way God the father has
dominion over all things in heaven, He gave
us to have dominion over all things on earth.
We are created to rule over everything that
lives on earth. Just like God the father is the
King He has made us kings over the earth.

The psalmist summarizes this thought very
well; Psalms 8:3-8. *" When I consider Your
heavens, the work of your fingers, The moon
and the stars, which You have ordained,
What is man that You are mindful of him,
And the son of man that you visit him? For
You have made him a little lower than the
angels, And You have crowned him with
glory and honour. You have made him to
have dominion over the works of your hands;
You have put all things under his feet, All*

*sheep and oxen- Even the beasts of the field,
The birds of the air, And the fish of the sea,
That pass through the paths of the seas."*

He has made us love beings just like He is a love being.

> *"Beloved, if God so loved us, we ought also to love one another."* (1John 4:11).

This scripture above shows us that like God, we also have the ability to love.

He has made us compassionate and merciful beings just like He is a compassionate and merciful being.

> *"Was it not right for you to have mercy on the other servant, even as I had mercy on you?"*
> (Matthew 18:33 BBE).

God the father made us merciful and compassionate beings just like He is merciful and compassionate.

God loves His image so much so that even after man fail into sin; when Adam and Eve his wife sinned. He did judge and condemn but went on looking for man.

God could not utterly destroy His image, but He went on looking and found him naked. God clothed them with leaves because they became naked as a result of sin.

In a bid not lose the crown of His creation forever, He ordered an angel to guard the entrance of the Garden of Eden so that Adam and Eve could not enter the garden and peradventure partake of the tree of life and remain evil forever. (Genesis 3:1-24).

When God the father destroyed the world during the time of Noah, He still reserved for

Himself a seed of His image in Noah and his family.

Due to the fact that He could not utterly destroy His image, He crafted a salvation plan to save His image from utter destruction that resulted from sin. For this reason God the father, chose to give His only begotten son to die in our place, so that He can preserve His image from utter destruction.

Satan hates the image of God with a passion, for this reason he will cause you to do vices which will destroy the image and likeness of God in you. He will make you feel useless, unimportant and unloved. He will cause you to destroy your life through drugs, prostitution and alcohol.

The devil is not happy that the Lord gave you such a place of dominion on earth, and therefore if you allow him, he will succeed in destroying the image and likeness of God in you.

Some of you have become strangers to yourselves now, you look at yourself in the mirror and all you see is a person you do not know. You ask yourself *"how did I get to this place?"I cannot love anymore; my body is scared or heavily tattooed?* **"How did I get to this place?" you ask**. It's the enemy, the devil, the hater and accuser of mankind who has made you that way. You have been courting the enemy and he has managed to make you hurt and hate yourself.

Maybe you do not know any better because the enemy started courting you when you were young? Maybe he made you believe that you are a homosexual, ugly and not worthy anything?

Maybe the enemy was courting your parents with drunkardness and drug abuse and you grew up in such an environment. And for that reason he started courting you in the manner similar to the way he courted your parents.

Remember the enemy comes to steal the likeness of God in you, to kill the life of God in you and to destroy the image of God in you. But it is never too late however deep your involvement with the enemy has been, however much the enemy thinks he has destroyed you, you have a chance to be redeemed from the snares of the enemy for Jesus came to redeem us from the power of the enemy and to give us back our image, likeness and life through the abundant life that He gives us.

> *"The thief cometh not, but for to steal, and to kill, and to destroy: I am come that they might have life, and that they might have it more abundantly."* (John 10:10).

Choose to exchange your life with the life of Christ Jesus, and then you will walk in the original plan of God for mankind and will share in the nature of God. Righteousness is the nature of God.

Prayer for wisdom to walk right

God of my Lord Jesus Christ, merciful Lord, by your Word, you created everything. By your wisdom you made man to rule over all creation, to govern the world with holiness and righteousness, to administer justice with integrity.
Give me the spirit of wisdom that sits besides your throne; give me a place among those who are sanctified.
I am your servant and I am only human, I am not strong and my life will be short without your

Word. I have little understanding of your word or how to apply it.

Even if a man is perfect in his ways, he will be thought of as nothing without the wisdom that comes from you.

You chose to die for me, on the cross so that I may know your ways. Wisdom is with you and knows your ways; He was present when you made the world. He knows what pleases you; what is right and in accordance to your commands.

Send the spirit of wisdom from your holy heavens, down from your glorious throne, so that He may work in my heart, and I may learn what pleases you.

He knows and understands everything, and will guide me wisely in everything I do. His glory will protect me and I will

walk wisely in everything I do;
then will my ways and deeds be
acceptable unto you. IN THE NAME
OF JESUS CHRIST I PRAY AMEN

Day Seventeen

Devotions for the day;

Morning sacrifice

Between   09:00hours to 10:00hours

Passage   Psalms 18:16 to 23; plus prayer for Wisdom

Noon sacrifice

Between   12:00hours to 13:00hours pm

Passage   Psalms 18: 24 to 32; plus prayer for Wisdom

Evening sacrifice

Between   15:00hours to 16:00hours

Passage   Psalms 18:33 to 40; plus prayer for Wisdom

Note: you should share the hour between the activities above according as you feel lead and if these times won't work for you please pick three separate hours of your own.

105

Day Eighteen

Devotions for the day;

Morning sacrifice

Between   09:00hours to 10:00hours

Passage   Psalms 18:41 to 50; plus prayer for
                   Wisdom

Noon sacrifice

Between   12:00hours to 13:00hours pm

Passage   Psalms 17: 1 to 8; plus prayer for
                   Wisdom

Evening sacrifice

Between   15:00hours to 16:00hours

Passage   Psalms 17:9 to 15; plus prayer for
                   Wisdom

Note: you should share the hour between the activities above according as you feel lead and if these times won't work for you please pick three separate hours of your own.

106

Day Nineteen

Grace pill no.7

You mean the world to God.

"What do you think? If a man owns a hundred sheep, and one of them wanders away, will he not leave the ninety-nine on the hills and go look for the one that wandered off?"
(Mathew 18:12 NIV).

$\mathscr{T}$he opening scripture above declares that like a shepherd or a father would leave the children who are home to go look for the one who is lost, the lord of heaven left and continues to leave those who are well to pursue those who are lost in drugs, sexual immorality, smoking, drunkardness with the hope of bringing them back home if they allow him.

> "What man of you, having an hundred sheep, if he lose one of them, doth not leave the ninety and nine in the wilderness, and go after that which is lost, until he find it?
> And when he hath found it, he layeth it on his shoulders, rejoicing. And when he cometh home, he calleth together his friends and neighbours, saying unto them, Rejoice with me; for I have found my sheep which was lost. I say unto you, that likewise joy shall be in heaven over one sinner that repenteth, more than over ninety and nine just persons, which need no repentance."   (Luke 15:4-7).

The scripture above further explains that when the master finds you He will put you on His shoulders meaning that He will carry you and give you rest from your struggles; rest from the addictions that you may be struggling with.

The only work He will expect of you is to stay put on His shoulders, the shoulders of His Word. Keep looking only unto Jesus who is the Word of God. Fill your heart and mind with the Word of God, and then rest in it.

The psalmist said it well when he declared that *"I hide your word in my heart that I may not sin against you."* You have to hide the Word of God in your heart so that you might not fall back into addictions.

"For he that is entered into his rest, he also hath ceased from his own works, as God did from his. Let us labour therefore (in studying and meditating on the Word of God) to enter into that rest, lest any man fall after the same example of unbelief." (Heb 4:10-11).

The Lord Jesus grieves over everyone one person, who dies in sin; who is arrested in drug addictions or any other addiction for that matter.

This is for the brother or sister who is lost in devise. The Lord is here looking out for you. Do not reject Him; do not ignore Him when He calls due to the shame that may result from your condition of sin.

Are you lost in sin; pornography, drug abuse, sexual addictions, homosexuality, lusts, witchcraft and Satanism? Do not despair you are of the prime importance to the Lord Jesus. He actually came to seek and save the lost. He is busy seeking for ways to reach your heart, so that He can save you from your addiction.

The Lord Jesus in Mathew 18:14 said He is not willing that you should be lost, it is not the will of God for you to be bound in sin.

The Lord is always making appeals to you time and again prompting you to make a decision for Him. He has spoken through your auntie, your mother, friends, stranger and even that pastor on television. He is doing everything and making every attempt through various people and circumstances so that you will not have an excuse when the Day of Judgment comes.

The Lord has not only stopped with appealing to your heart but has also preserved your life and showed you mercy time and again. *Remember how disaster by passed you and hit your immediate neighbor? How you survived that car accident? Or how your life was spared in unexplainable circumstances?* And many other ways He has been showing signals to you that sometimes make you acknowledge an invisible hand of protection.

The world calls this being lucky or fortunate, but don't be foolish and ignore these signals because they are judgment matters. The Lord will remind you of the attempts and signals of mercy and protection he showed you during your lifetime.

The Lord is not really being slow about His promises to return, as some people may think, No! He is being patient for your sake. He does not want anyone to perish, so He is giving more time for everyone to repent. (2 Peter 3:9).

Brothers and sisters the Lord is patiently waiting for you to repent, before He comes. This is because He does not want you to die in your sins. He is waiting for you to make a decision for Him because He has already paid the full price for your sins.

Why should you die for the sin that is already paid for?

He loves you so much, and that's why He pursues you, because He has already paid for the sin that keeps tormenting you. He wants to set you free from that sin and addiction and give you a life that full of peace, love and joy!

You are worth the Lord's Life. Even if you were the only one on earth, He would still have died to save you from your sins and addictions.

Prayer for wisdom to walk right

God of my Lord Jesus Christ, merciful Lord, by your word, you created everything. By your wisdom you made man to rule over all creation, to govern the world with holiness and righteousness, to administer justice with integrity.
Give me the spirit of wisdom that sits besides your throne; give me a place among those who are sanctified.
I am your servant and I am only human, I am not strong and my life will be short without your word. I have little understanding of your word or how to apply it.
Even if a man is perfect in his ways, he will be thought of as nothing without the wisdom that comes from you.

114

You chose to die for me, on the
cross so that I may know your
ways. Wisdom is with you and
knows your ways; He was present
when you made the world. He
knows what pleases you; what is
right and in accordance to your
commands.
Send the spirit of wisdom from
your holy heavens, down from
your glorious throne, so that
she may work in my heart, and I
may learn what pleases you.
He knows and understands
everything, and will guide
wisely in everything I do. His
glory will protect me and I will
walk wisely in everything I do;
then will my ways and deeds be
acceptable unto you. IN THE NAME
OF JESUS CHRIST I PRAY AMEN

Day Twenty

Devotions for the day;

Morning sacrifice

Between   09:00hours to 10:00hours

Passage   Psalms 118:1 to 10; plus prayer for Wisdom

Noon sacrifice

Between   12:00hours to 13:00hours pm

Passage   Psalms 118: 11 to 20; plus prayer for Wisdom

Evening sacrifice

Between   15:00hours to 16:00hours

Passage   Psalms 118:21 to 29; plus prayer for Wisdom

Note: you should share the hour between the activities above according as you feel lead and if these times won't work for you please pick three separate hours of your own.

Day Twenty-One

Devotions for the day;

Morning sacrifice

Between   09:00hours to 10:00hours

Passage   John 3:1 to 8; plus prayer for
Wisdom

Noon sacrifice

Between   12:00hours to 13:00hours pm

Passage   John 1: 10 to 18; plus prayer for
Wisdom

Evening sacrifice

Between   15:00hours to 16:00hours

Passage 2 Corinthians 5:14 to 21 plus prayer
For Wisdom

*Note: you should share the hour between the activities above
according as you feel lead and if these times won't work for you
please pick three separate hours of your own.*

117

Day Twenty-Two

Grace pill no.8

You are not condemned.

"For God did not send his son into the world to condemn the world, but to save the world through him."

(John 3:17 NIV).

*M*any folks around the world view God as the judge and condemner of their sinful lives, they see Him as the one who doesn't want them to enjoy life this may be true on one hand but He did not come to condemn the world this time around. After this time of grace is gone, for sure He will come to judge and condemn all sin.

The main reason why God sent His son Jesus to this world was because of the love that He has for the world. The motivation for sending His son was not to condemn but to save and give eternal life.

> *"For God so loved the world that He gave His only begotten Son, that whoever believes in Him should not perish but have everlasting life"* (John 3:16 NIV).

From the above scripture we can see that the reason the Lord God sent His Son into the world was because of His love for the world. He sent His Son in response to His love for the world, and not for His hatred for sin.

As the opening scripture rightly puts it, Jesus did not come to judge us for our sin neither did He come to condemn us for our

119

sin and addictions, but He came to save us, to deliver us from our sins and addictions.

Many folks around the world feel condemned each time they hear someone talking about Jesus. It's wrong to feel condemned at the mention of the Name of Jesus. Maybe someone condemned you and relegated you as an outcast in the Name of the Lord and from then on you fill condemned at that name?

I have good news for you; whatever your parents, church or friends may have said to you does not matter. What matters is that Jesus, the one who paid for your sins does not condemn you! He came to save you from your accusers and give you grace and the ability not to sin anymore.

"When Jesus had lifted up himself, and saw none but the woman, he said unto her, Woman, where are those thine accusers? hath no man condemned thee? She said, No man, Lord. And Jesus said unto her, Neither do I condemn thee: go, and sin no more."

(John 8:10).

This woman, brothers and sisters was caught in the very act of committing adultery. There was no need for a trial to ascertain whether she was guilty or not because she was caught red-handed.

Did she deserve condemnation? Yes she did! Did people condemn her? Yes they did! Did they accuse her? Yes they did! Was she wrong? Yes she was!

Maybe you also deserve to be accused and condemned? Maybe many people have already accused and condemned you? Just like He did for the woman who was caught in the very act of adultery, Jesus does not condemn you. He sees the original plan for you and in you, every time He looks at you. He does not look at you through the glasses of the sin or addiction you are battling with.

Jesus Christ the great physician came to this world particularly for you, the sick, so that He can take away your spiritual sickness which is sin. A Doctor comes specifically for the sick, to give them treatment for their sickness; the doctor does not come to condemn the sick and their sickness. He comes to give hope to the hopeless.

"When Jesus heard it, he saith unto them, they that are whole have no need of the physician, but they that are sick: I came not to call the righteous, but sinners to repentance." (Mark 2:17).

For this reason the Lord Jesus came to this world, to heal the sickness of sin. As the opening scripture puts it, He did not send His Son to condemn the world but to save the world through Him. Jesus is the great physician who came especially because of our sickness, to save us from the sickness of sin and not to condemn us.

The same way Doctors are Doctors because of the sick, Jesus is the Christ because of our sins and addictions. The same way Doctors give hope to the sick and not

123

condemnation, the Lord Jesus gives hope of eternal life to this dyeing world.

Do not feel condemned because of the talk about Jesus Christ our Lord; on the contrary you should feel a wonderful hope!

Prayer for strength in the inner man

For this reason I bow my knees to the father of our Lord Jesus Christ, of whom the whole family in heaven and earth in named after and ask in prayer:
Dear righteous father, may You grant me, according to the richness in your glory, strength by the power of the Holy Spirit in the man of my heart; that Christ Jesus may be evident in my life by faith, that I may be rooted and grounded in love. That I may be able to understand with all the other saints what

124

is the breadth, and the length
and the depth and the height of
the love of God; so that I may
know the love of Christ which
surpasses all understanding.
That I may be filled with the
full measure of godliness in my
life. IN THE NAME OF JESUS
CHRIST I PRAY AMEN.

Day Twenty-Three

Devotions for the day;

Morning sacrifice

Between   09:00hours to 10:00hours

Passage   John 5:19 to 27; plus prayer for
Strength

Noon sacrifice

Between   12:00hours to 13:00hours pm

Passage   John 8: 28 to 36; plus prayer for
Strength

Evening sacrifice

Between   15:00hours to 16:00hours

Passage   John 10:1 to 11; plus prayer for
Strength

Note: you should share the hour between the activities above according as you feel lead and if these times won't work for you please pick three separate hours of your own.

Day Twenty-Four

Devotions for the day;

Morning sacrifice

Between   09:00hours to 10:00hours

Passage   Romans 8:1 to 10; plus prayer for Strength

Noon sacrifice

Between   12:00hours to 13:00hours pm

Passage   Romans: 11 to 20; plus prayer for Strength

Evening sacrifice

Between   15:00hours to 16:00hours

Passage   Romans 8:21 to 39; plus prayer for Strength

Note: you should share the hour between the activities above according as you feel lead and if these times won't work for you please pick three separate hours of your own.

Day Twenty-Five

Grace pill no.9

Identifying sin in your life.

"The heart is deceitful above all things, And desperately wicked; Who can know it? I, the Lord, search the heart, I test the mind, Even to give every man according to his ways, According to the fruit of his doings." (Jeremiah 17:8-9 NKJV).

𝓘 remember the one night after finishing with my routing studying and meditating on the Word of God. I asked the Lord to take me to His holy hill; I was meditating on psalms 24.

After spending minutes of seeking the Lord, I saw in a vision a great light, this light was so strong such that I stopped looking up to avoid the light. The light brought a sense of dirtiness in me. I felt so dirty, such that I almost could not handle the filthy I felt on me.

Suddenly a saw in a vision my heart, like a great file with lots of folders. Then I saw this man opening the folders one after another. Each folder had some filth and dirty things in it. The first folder was opened, and immediately I remembered the sins I committed when I was in high school. The second folder was opened and I remembered the hatred I had harbored from my high school days, the unforgiveness, the pain, the shame and the anger.

Folders after folders were opened and I spent over 3 hours confessing the sins that I had committed years back and had forgotten about.

From that moment on, the opening scripture made a lot of sense to me, I felt like a new light was shed on the scripture I knew for some time. I realized that my behaviour was controlled by the sin that was sitted in the compartments of my heart. Then I realized that the world is missing the point on the subject of identifying sin in a person's life.

Man has had problems from the beginning of time to identify the root of sin in their lives. Many still do not know why they like to do the things they do. Until the real root of sin is identified, the fight against sin and addictions still remains a losing battle.

The world has come up with lots of therapies to fight addictions and sin. They have rehabilitation centers to try and rehabilitate people from their sinful nature, how is that possible? How can a person rehabilitate another person from his very nature? The world rehabilitates people's behaviours and not their hearts. They deal with the results and not the cause.

How many people know the dangers of doing certain things but keep on doing them? How many Doctors understand and can even explain to you the dangers of smoking, but they themselves are chain smokers?

Let me tell you something, every person loves themselves. That's the reason why they always want the best for themselves. But why do people do things, they know will jeopardize their healthy and can even cause them death? Don't tell me they don't care because they do!

The opening scripture gives light into the root of sin and addictions in our lives; the heart is the workshop of sin in peoples' lives.

131

The heart that is not renewed has a great affinity for sin; the opening scripture shows us that the heart is desperately wicked. It always lust for evil. For as long as man keeps on looking for sin in wrong places he is bound to be a slave of sin and addictions.

Many people think that if they stop going to certain places and remain at home alone, they will not sin. Others put the blame on other people and things. A Person on his own and along can contemplate evil in his hearts as much as a person who finds himself in places which are prone to sin.

A place or situation only avails your heart a chance to do what it premeditated. For as long as the heart is not pure, everything it sees will be interpreted into evil. *"To the pure all things are pure and to the impure all things are impure."* (Titus1:15).

The heart of man always directs the ways of man; it is the heart that determines how your day will be, what kinds of friends you have and ultimately the life you to live. The heart is the ruler of the will of man. That is the reason why a person can do almost anything for a loved one.

This then means that if your heart is rooted in immorality, there is nothing you can do but be immoral. If you are rooted in materialism you will do anything to get your way. This applies to every area of our lives; the Lord by His Spirit spoke through the prophet Jeremiah in 7:24 said this; *"Yet they did not obey or incline their ear, but followed the counsels and the dictates of the their evil hearts, and went backward and not forward."*

The Lord through his prophet used the word "dictate" to symbolize the power of the heart over our actions; the heart dictates our

133

ways and works, that is the reason why the Lord in the opening scripture said I search the heart, I test the mind; Even to give everyman according to his ways, ...According to the fruit of his doings.

The Lord God in His wisdom has given us the two areas of our lives where sin and addictions are manufactured, the area of our mind which controls our ways of thinking and ways of doing things and the heart which controls the things we do. For this reason the Lord searches the heart to see whether there is good or evil in our lives, thereby knowing the outcome our lives; whether freedom or addiction.

> *"Guard your heart all diligence for out of it springs the issue of life."* (Proverbs 4: 23).

Sin comes and settles in our lives through the things we read, things we watch and the things we talk about among others. These things have the ability to corrupt our hearts. Therefore if we guard our hearts by choosing what we watch, what we talk about and the books we read we'll protect hearts from sin and addictions.

> *"A good man out of the good treasure of his heart brings forth good things, and an evil man out of the evil treasure brings forth evil things."*
> (Mathew 12: 48).

Sin is found in the heart and therefore must be dealt with from the heart. The deeds, works and behaviours are just the fruits of what is in your heart.

To completely do away with sin and addictions one needs to purify their hearts with the washing by the Word of God, through studying and meditating on the Holy Scriptures.

Prayer for strength in the inner man

For this reason I bow my knees to the father of our Lord Jesus Christ, of whom the whole family in heaven and earth in named after and ask in prayer:
Dear righteous father, may You grant me, according to the richness in your glory strength by the power of the Holy Spirit in the man of my heart; that Christ Jesus may be evident in my life by faith, that I may be rooted and grounded in love. That I may be able to understand with all the other saints what

is the breadth, and the length
and the depth and the height of
the love of God; so that I may
know the love of Christ which
surpasses all understanding.
That I may be filled with the
full measure of godliness in my
life. IN THE NAME OF JESUS
CHRIST I PRAY AMEN.

Day Twenty-Six

Devotions for the day;

Morning sacrifice

Between   09:00hours to 10:00hours

Passage 2 Corinthians 10: 3 to 8; plus prayer
For Strength

Noon sacrifice

Between   12:00hours to 13:00hours pm

Passage   Ephesians 6: 10 to 18; plus prayer
For Strength

Evening sacrifice

Between   15:00hours to 16:00hours

Passage   Ephesians 1:17 to 23; plus prayer
For Strength

Note: you should share the hour between the activities above according as you feel lead and if these times won't work for you please pick three separate hours of your own.

Day Twenty-Seven

Devotions for the day;

Morning sacrifice

Between   09:00hours to 10:00hours

Passage   Ephesians 1:1 to 7; plus prayer for
Strength

Noon sacrifice

Between   12:00hours to 13:00hours pm

Passage   Ephesians 1: 8 to 14; plus prayer for
Strength

Evening sacrifice

Between   15:00hours to 16:00hours

Passage   Ephesians 3:14 to 21; plus prayer
For Strength

*Note: you should share the hour between the activities above
according as you feel lead and if these times won't work for you
please pick three separate hours of your own.*

Day Twenty-Eight

Grace pill no.10

How to overcome Sin and Addictions in your life.

"I have hidden your word in my heart that I might not sin against you."
(Psalm 119:11 NIV).

*M*any people world over have tried many things to cure the problem of sin and addictions, but have failed. Many have tried a lot of ways to overcome this sickness but all in vein. Many pastors and teachers of the Word of God have in ignorance made this problem even worse. In an effort to overcome sin they have condemned the people who live in sin and struggling with addictions from the

140

pulpit. Without knowing they have caused the sinners and addicts to meditate on their addictions with the hope of overcoming it, but only succeeding to give the sin and addiction more power over their lives.

The scriptures call the law the ministry of condemnation. This ministry of condemning may sound good, as people may say that this pastor is uncompromising, he does not tolerates sinners in the church. But one thing he is missing is that he is preaching the law, and the law is the ministry of death, the ministry that gives sin power.

> *"But if the ministration of death, written and engraven in stones ….."* (2Corinthians 3:7).

> *"The sting of death is sin; and the strength of sin is the law."* (1Corinthians 15:56).

One truth men of God should never forget is that whenever they are preach the law and condemn the people because of sin; they are ministering death to their members. They are strengthening the power or grip of sin over their members' lives. The Lord Jesus did not come to condemn because He did not bring the law but grace and truth.

> **"For the law was given by Moses, but grace and truth came by Jesus Christ."**
> (John 1:17).

The opening scripture gives us the ancient truth that is still in force today. This truth is the solution to the whole problem of sin and addictions. The Psalmist declared in truth that *"I hide your Word in my heart that I might not sin against you."* Why did the spsalmist hide God's Word in his heart? Why did he

142

admonish us to hide the Word of God in our hearts?

This is because the Word of God has the ability to burn out the sin from the heart and the power to break the rock solid bondage of addiction into pieces. **(Jeremiah 23: 29).** The Word of God also has power to divide the soul and spirit, and joints and marrows and it can discern the thoughts and intentions of the heart. **(Hebrews 4: 12).**

The Word knows your heart and exposes every area of your heart where sin is present. Remember the vision I had and shared about how my heart was exposed, it all happened after a long period in days and months of continual studying and meditating on the Word of God.

At that moment the Word of God exposed the areas of sin in my heart, it even exposed a lot of sin which I had no memory of at that

143

time. The Word also has the power to wash every area of your heart clean so that you are spotless and blameless. **(Ephesians 5: 26).**

> *"Now ye are clean through the word which I have spoken unto you."*
>
> (John 15:3).

It's only the Word of grace that can totally remove and clean a person from sin and addiction. The Lord Jesus in John 8: 32 declared that the only thing that can free a person from sin and addictions is the truth. The scripture declares *"Then you will know the truth, and the truth will set you free."* In John 17: 17 the Lord declared as He was praying for us to the father that the Word is truth. *"Sanctify (cleanse) them by Your truth, Your Word is truth."*

Only the Word of God can cleanse a person from sin and addictions. The Word of God if studied and meditated upon has the power to break the strongholds of sin and addictions in a person's life. It has the power to sanctify you spirit, soul and body, thereby removing any trace of sin and addiction in your life. Go for the Word and you will be free from your addictions.

Men of God should restrain from teaching the law because the law brings condemnation and thereby give sin power. Grace on the other hand, gives people dominion over sin; it is the Word of grace that gives people the power over sin and addictions.

The Lord Jesus said in John 15: 3 and made it clear that we can only be made clean by the Word He has spoken. And we know that the Words of our Lord Jesus are full of grace; like for instance the story of the woman caught in

145

adultery as recorded in the book of John 8:3-11. The Lord Jesus unlike the people who operated by the Law of Moses, did not condemn her but had grace on her and asked her to go and sin no more.

The Words *"go and sin no more"* gave her the power over sin, these Words of grace can clean a person from sin and give then dominion over it.

> *"She said, No man, Lord. And Jesus said unto her, Neither do I condemn thee: go, and sin no more."*   (John 8:11).

Beloved let us give our flock the pure Word of grace which is able to clean them, build them and give them an inheritance among the saints (Acts 20:32). Let us restrain from condemning them with the law and further deepen them into sin and addictions.

As for you my brother or sister, who is struggling with addictions; Study and meditate on the Word of God daily and your problem of sin and addiction will vanish. Do not even force yourself to stop instantly the sinful habits, but just be diligent with your study of the Word and you will notice a change in you.

After a little while of studying and meditating on the Word of God, substitute your lust for sin with the Word of God. When you feel the lust for sex, drugs, masturbation or whatever addiction you are struggling with, go for the Word instead and you will find rest from your bondage of sin and addiction. To the glory of the Lord!

Prayer for strength in the inner man

For this reason I bow my knees
to the father of our Lord Jesus
Christ, of whom the whole family
in heaven and earth in named
after and ask in prayer:
Dear righteous father, may You
grant me, according to the
richness in your glory strength
by the power of the Holy Spirit
in the man of my heart; that
Christ Jesus may be evident in
my life by faith, that I may be
rooted and grounded in love.
That I may be able to understand
with all the other saints what
is the breadth, and the length
and the depth and the height of
the love of God; so that I may
know the love of Christ which
surpasses all understanding.
That I may be filled with the
full measure of godliness in my

148

life.   IN   THE   NAME   OF   JESUS CHRIST I PRAY AMEN.

Day Twenty-Nine

Devotions for the day;

Morning sacrifice
Between   09:00hours to 10:00hours

Passage   Ephesians 4:22 to 32; plus prayer
For Strength

Noon sacrifice
Between   12:00hours to 13:00hours pm

Passage   Romans 12: 1 to 10; plus prayer for
Strength

Evening sacrifice
Between   15:00hours to 16:00hours

Passage   Romans 12:11 to 21; plus prayer for
Strength

Note: you should share the hour between the activities above according as you feel lead and if these times won't work for you please pick three separate hours of your own.

Day Thirty

Devotions for the day;

Morning sacrifice

Between   09:00hours to 10:00hours

Passage   Isaiah 33:1 to 24; plus prayer for
                  Strength

Noon sacrifice

Between   12:00hours to 13:00hours pm

Passage   Isaiah 41: 1 to 29; plus prayer for
                  Strength

Evening sacrifice

Between   15:00hours to 16:00hours

Passage   Isaiah 42:1 to 25; plus prayer for
                  Strength

Note: you should share the hour between the activities above according as you feel lead and if these times won't work for you please pick three separate hours of your own.

151

Manifested to destroy Sin and Addictions.

"........for this purpose the son of God was manifested, that He might destroy the works of the devil." (1 John 3:8 NKJV).

*J*esus Christ is the son of God who was manifested to destroy the works of the devil in our lives. Many times we struggle with a lot of sinful addictions in our lives and are often made hopeless by them. But I have good news for you; the son of God was manifested to destroy all the addictions that have kept you in bondage.

152

When Jesus manifests in your life, He will destroy all the works of the enemy in your life. This is the reason why He came to this earth some 2000 years ago. He came to destroy all the works of the enemy in this world, once and for all.

I know some folks would get confused as to how can Christ be manifested in our lives when He already has gone to heaven? Precious people we need to realize that the Lord Jesus is the Word of God that became flesh and dwelt among us **(John 1:14)**.

The Lord Jesus is the personal Word of God and the scriptures; the bible is the written Word of God. The two are one, but are manifested differently. One was manifested as a living person; the other is manifested as the living Word.

153

All we need to do brothers and sisters is to set our hearts on seeking Him, through studying of the Word of God. The Lord Jesus is the living Word of God, therefore the more we seek Him in his Word, the more He manifests Himself in us and the more He destroys the works of the enemy in our lives.

When His Word is manifested in your life, it will destroy all the sinful addictions that have kept you in bondage. The Amplified version of the bible explains the opening scripture this way: *"...........The reason the son of God was made manifest (visible) was to undo (destroy, loosen and dissolve) the works the devil (has done).*

This scripture shows that, as the effects of the Word of God become visible in your life, it will destroy all the works of the enemy in your life and that includes; sinful lusts and addictions. The Word will loosen all the strongholds that have kept you as a slave of sinful addictions. It will also dissolve all the hindrances and mountains that have kept you from your freedom.

The biggest labour you need to do is to diligently study and meditate on the Word of God. When the Word of God is full in your heart, it will manifest itself in your life, it will be visible in your life to destroy and dissolve all the sinful and addictive habits. The scripture in Ecclesiastes 11:3 declares that *"if the clouds are full of rain, they empty themselves upon the earth..."*

This scripture encourages us to concentrate on studying and meditating on the Word and when it is full, the Word itself will work in you to destroy every work of the enemy in your life.

Notes

This medicine bottle will work if you work it. It will be meaningless if you do not go through this bottle with faith. Faith is the substance of things hoped, and evidence of things not seen. So without faith the freedom you hope for will not come to pass.

If you have not fully received your freedom by the end of the 30days period of the bottle, you are free to start again from the start. The Word of God is always in the present, because it's eternal.

You can also use the bottle for your own Spiritual growth; it contains a lot of insight into the heart of Grace. You can use it for teaching others about the mind of God towards people living in sin.

Progress Indicators Notes

The progress indicators notes segment is a provision given for you to record your weekly progress. The progress testimonies you write each week will act as a reminder of the addictions you've overcome in the previous weeks. This will help you resolve not to go back to the habits you've already overcome.

Week one

....
....
....
....
....
....
....
....
....
....

Week two

....
....
....
....
....
....
....
....
....
....

Week three

....
....
....
....
....
....
....

....

....

Week four

....

....

....

....

....

....

....

....

....

....

If you need prayer support or someone to talk to before and during the therapy please contact us at: medicinebottle @gmail.com or musagmwanza@yahoo.com.

Inviting Musa George Mwanza to your area

Musa George Mwanza may be available to speak at your church, conference, or crusade. Please contact us with the details of your ministry and your invitation. You must also give information of the nature of the event. Musa and his team will pray over your invitation and respond to you as soon as possible.

Musa George Mwanza
P.O Box 1015
Jeffrey's Bay 6330,
Eastern Cape
South Africa.

E-mail: musagmwanza@yahoo.com